BLS WORKING PAPERS

U.S. DEPARTMENT OF LABOR
Bureau of Labor Statistics

OFFICE OF COMPENSATION AND
WORKING CONDITIONS

Compensation Supplements and Use of Incentive Pay in U.S. Job Markets

Anthony J. Barkume, U.S. Bureau of Labor Statistics

Working Paper 352
February 2002

The views expressed are those of the author and do not necessarily reflect the policies of the U.S. Bureau of Labor Statistics or the views of other staff members.

Compensation Supplements and Use of Incentive Pay in US Job Markets

Anthony J. Barkume[*]
Compensation Research and Program Development Group
U.S. Bureau of Labor Statistics

October 2001

---

[*] I wish to thank Al Schwenk for preparing the data extract used in this paper and Will Carrington, Dave Kaplan, and Brooks Pierce for their comments and suggestions on preliminary research. The views expressed in this paper are those of the author and do not reflect the policies of the U.S. Bureau of Labor Statistics. An earlier version of this paper was presented at the 1999 Southern Economics Association meetings.

Abstract of
"Compensation Supplements and Use of Incentive Pay in US Job Markets"

Anthony J. Barkume
U.S. Bureau of Labor Statistics

The firm's interest in monitoring and/or motivating workers appears to be an important reason why firms use pay supplements such as bonuses and overtime work. Using a representative sample of U.S. private industry jobs, this paper obtains some indirect evidence on what pay supplements serve as incentive instruments. I study how various pay supplements differ in both incidence and generosity when traditional incentive pay--pay based on individual results such as piece rates or sales commissions--is a part of job earnings. If a firm does use incentive pay the marginal benefit of a pay supplement <u>as an incentive instrument</u> should fall. Otherwise, the use of incentive pay should have no necessary relationship to provision of a pay supplement, with provision driven by worker preferences for the benefits provided.

The paper's methodology follows that in Richard Freeman's 1981 study of union-nonunion differences in compensation supplements. (Since the data I use includes union status, I also update Freeman's results.) Specifically, I estimate expected employer costs per hour worked for various compensation supplements. Across all US private industry jobs, employer costs for bonuses not based on individual results are about half of predicted levels with use of incentive pay. Similarly, use of incentive pay reduces expected employer spending levels in defined contribution retirement plans by about a third. Employer spending on health insurance was unrelated to use of incentive pay but forty percent higher in union jobs. Union jobs had more costly compensation supplements, except for employer payments for bonuses and to defined contribution retirement plans.

The results also suggest that use of incentive pay and collective bargaining help to accommodate differences in worker preferences for hours of work. Among jobs with the same fulltime year-round work schedule, I estimate that a slightly higher amount of expected overtime work is attached to a union job. But a worker choosing between full time jobs offering paid leave can also expect about six fewer work days per year in a union job than in a job using incentive pay.

Anthony J. Barkume
Compensation Research and Program Development Group
U.S. Bureau of Labor Statistics
2 Massachusetts Ave., N.E.
Postal Square Building, room 4130
Washington, D.C. 20212
(202) 691-7527 ; e-mail: barkume_a@bls.gov

I. Introduction: Motivation and Plan of Paper

Traditional incentive pay--pay based on individual results using a predetermined formula such as piece rates or sales commissions—embeds high-powered incentives directly into worker compensation. Substantial earnings premiums have been found with use of incentive pay in narrowly defined occupations even after controlling for worker characteristics (Booth and Frank (1999)) or a switch in pay regime (Lazear (2000b)). Most recent analysis of these earnings premiums has investigated whether workers taking incentive pay jobs use greater work effort or have greater ability[1], since firms using incentive pay would face higher labor costs unless workers in incentive pay jobs also had higher productivity.

However, an earnings premium with use of incentive pay could also be consistent with all firms offering the same total employee compensation for a particular job. Equality of total employee compensation across firms could be possible if <u>supplemental</u> employer compensation, such as cash bonuses, paid leave, overtime pay and employee benefits, is systematically lower when the firm chooses to use incentive pay in employee governance. The purpose of this paper is to investigate the relationship between compensation supplements and use of incentive pay in a recent representative cross section of the U.S. job market.

Section II develops the argument that if supplemental compensation has value to the firm as an incentive instrument[2] to monitor and motivate employees, this value falls if the firm chooses to also use incentive pay. Although substitution between types of incentive instruments can not be directly observed, the cross section data I use can compare the effects of incentive pay use on different types of supplemental compensation. For example, if health insurance does not provide the firm an incentive

---

[1] Lazear (2000a) shows how work effort and ability could interact in workers sorting into jobs using incentive pay.
[2] Holmstrom and Milgrom (1994) emphasize that the firm has three classes of incentive instruments to govern the employment relationship: (1) direct payments based on employee activity, (2) asset co-ownership (equity stakes), and (3) the job design itself, selecting production techniques and systems for monitoring work. Our analysis is limited to the first class of incentive instruments.

instrument, use of incentive pay by the firm should not affect employer provision of health insurance, all other things being equal.

To make these comparisons, I use a representative sample of U.S. private industry jobs in March 1997 used in production of the Employment Cost Index (ECI) program. Pierce (2001) uses ECI data to study the evolution of compensation inequality in the US job market. The empirical approach follows Freeman (1980), who used establishment data to study union-nonunion differences in supplemental compensation. Since the ECI sample data set in this paper also includes whether collective bargaining is used in the individual job, the study also updates Freeman's findings on union-nonunion differences in supplemental compensation and contrasts them with the incentive pay differences. Section III provides the details on sample data characteristics and Section IV develops the methodology for estimating expected differences in supplemental compensation with use of incentive pay, controlling for detailed occupation and total compensation of the job as well as the establishment size and industry of the employer.

Section V presents the results. As expected, bonuses not based on individual results and use of overtime work were found to be substantially lower when incentive pay is used on the job. For example, when incentive pay is used employer expenditures on bonuses are predicted to be 46 percent of the level otherwise expected among all US private industry full time jobs. I also found that expected hours of holiday/vacation leave and employer spending on defined contribution retirement plans were both lower with use of incentive pay, suggesting a role for worker preferences in these job market outcomes. Not all types of supplemental compensation were found to be related to use of incentive pay; the provision and generosity of both health insurance and defined benefit retirement plans are not significantly different across all US private industry jobs when incentive pay is used. Consistent with Freeman's earlier results, we find that union jobs have substantially higher expected spending on all supplemental compensation except on cash bonuses and on defined contribution retirement plans.

We conclude the paper with some speculations about how the interaction of employer motives and worker preferences can explain the findings of substantial differences in hours of work between incentive pay and union jobs. Incentive pay jobs may attract workers with preferences for higher work hours (lower demands for leisure) since accrual of paid leave in the work schedule provides a means to generate higher hours of work. If a hypothetical worker in US private industry chose a job using incentive pay instead of a union job, then the results predict that the worker could obtain an additional fulltime week of work per year, even when both jobs offer the same year round forty hour week work schedule. However, attached to the offer of a union job is a higher amount of overtime work than in nonunion jobs.

II. Supplemental Compensation and Use of Incentive Pay

Some types of supplemental compensation can help the firm to motivate and/or monitor workers. Besides the obvious incentive role of overtime premiums, paid vacation or sick leave may provide an instrument to monitor absenteeism and coordinate work schedules[3], and group bonuses (including, but not limited to, profit-sharing) can encourage teamwork in the workplace. Also, pensions can provide an implicit performance bond to workers to promote the formation of firm-specific capital (see Ippolito (1997)).

If a particular type of supplemental compensation can help the firm to govern the employment relationship, it should have less value to the firm when using incentive pay. Starting with Williamson (1975), when the nature of the job or the work setting makes it feasible, payment based on individual results has been characterized as a "high powered" incentive.[4] With incentive pay, tenure or reliability considerations are less important to the employer. Deferred compensation is less important to workers or the firm because there is no need to bargain over the returns to job-specific human capital; workers are paid on their results regardless of whether these results could be replicated in other firms. Monitoring is less important because, as Pencavel (1977) notes, incentive pay provides employers an automatic "on-the-job screening" capability because earnings are adjusted

---

[3] See, for example, Reisenweitz (1997).
[4] Of course, as Lazear (2000) stresses, many other compensation schemes can be high-powered in the appropriate work setting. Lazear stresses the value of incentive pay to sort those in a heterogeneous work force with the greatest productivity to their most efficient employment.

for variations in productivity and effort between employees. Thus, use of incentive pay in job compensation should be associated with lower incidence and/or generosity for paid leave, retirement benefits, or other compensation supplements that the firm would have otherwise used in employee governance.

If use of incentive pay lowers the share of supplemental compensation in total employee compensation, earnings premiums with incentive pay overstate corresponding premiums in total employee compensation. Using various samples from the BLS Industry Wage Surveys of earnings in narrowly defined occupations within the same industry, a variety of different studies have found an earnings premium for piece rate pay of eight to ten percent[5]. Later analysis of household data sets having broader job coverage--but also having less precise information on method of pay--are also consistent with the earlier results using direct job comparisons; see Booth and Frank (1999) and Parent (1999). However, a significant limitation to this earnings premium research has been lack of data on total employee compensation. Instead, individual cash earnings in piece rate jobs have been compared to the straight time (that is, exclusive of bonuses, overtime, or shift differentials) wage rate in jobs not using piece rates.

The aggregate data from the ECI program indicate that an earnings premium for piece rate pay could even be consistent with the absence of an incentive pay differential in total employee compensation. Published data, shown in Table 1, show that employer costs for supplemental compensation (termed "Benefit Costs" in the ECI program) are a large share of total employee compensation among blue-collar worker occupations where piece rate pay is more prevalent. Excluding costs for "Legally Required Benefits" (employer payroll taxes, workers' compensation insurance), costs for supplemental compensation were $3.26 per hour worked among Machine Operators, Assemblers, and Inspectors in March 2001. If a ten percent premium for straight-time pay in incentive pay jobs in this occupational group was offset by $1.34 less in supplemental compensation, there would be no differential in total employee compensation with incentive pay.

---

[5] See Brown (1992), King (1975), Mitchell, Lewin, and Lawler (1990), Petersen (1992), and Seiler (1984).

In contrast, Freeman (1981) found that because supplemental compensation is a greater share of total compensation in union jobs, the union premium in straight time pay understated the total compensation per hour differential. Using data for larger firms, Freeman estimated, for U.S. private industry as a whole, a straight-time pay per hour union premium of 15.9 percent but a total compensation per hour differential of 18.8 percent, reflecting the larger share of pay supplements in union compensation.[6] Freeman hypothesized that this difference reflected the greater importance of average worker preferences in the collective bargaining process, assuming that the average worker would have a higher demand for benefits than would marginal workers.

III. Data Characteristics

To examine the empirical association between incentive pay and supplemental compensation, I used a March 1997 cross-section of ECI micro data (with the job as the unit of observation). To produce the ECI, detailed information is collected at the employer's establishment on individual earnings as well as on employer expenditures for various elements of supplemental compensation, including employee benefits. Expenditures on supplemental compensation are intended as a measure of the expected payments attached to sample jobs, reflecting the usual amounts that would be accrued per hour worked over the work year (e.g., usual overtime hours worked per year, usual hours of paid sick leave taken over the year). Data on characteristics such as the detailed occupation of the job, the industry of the employing establishment, the establishment size, and whether the job is full time or covered by a collective bargaining agreement, are also obtained for each sampled job. Pierce (2001) uses ECI micro data to study the evolution of inequality of total employee compensation in the U.S. job market.

Although not now used in published ECI series, ECI data collection includes an indicator whether incentive pay is used in sample jobs.[7] The incentive pay indicator captures jobs where straight-time wages or salaries "...are tied, at least in part, to

---

[6] See Freeman (1981, p.504); I am reporting the antilogs of the log differentials that Freeman presented.
[7] For more information on the incentive pay classification and evidence that the presence of incentive pay provisions increases the time series volatility of the ECI, see Barkume and Moehrele (2001).

commissions, production bonuses, piece rates, or other individual incentives"[8] and excludes profit-sharing distributions, all-employee payments, or other "nonproduction bonuses" because the latter payments are not directly linked to the individual worker's efforts. However, jobs in which tip income is customary are not classified as including incentive pay because the employer incurs no direct cost. Since tip income also provides high-powered incentives but cannot be identified in the ECI data, I excluded sample observations in selected service occupations[9] in which I expected tip income to be prevalent.

The ECI sample data do have some limitations linking compensation with use of incentive pay. Individual worker characteristics are not obtained in ECI data collection and all data records are job averages (e.g., average pay across all job incumbents). Also not retained in the permanent data files is the proportion of straight-time pay derived from the incentive pay formula, or whether the incentive pay formula is based on sales (e.g., commissions) or production (e.g., piece rates). However, incentive pay formulas usually reflect commissions among sales and managerial[10] occupations and piece rates or other production bonuses among skilled production workers. Thus, additional separate comparisons were made among these two occupational groups.

Summary descriptions of the data for the March 1997 cross section are shown in Table 2. Sample sizes are the numbers of jobs sampled while the means and standard deviations reflect the employment weights of sample jobs. (The use of sample design information in estimation is discussed below.) Because past research indicates that part-time employment reduces both compensation levels and supplemental compensation[11], the samples were restricted to jobs with full time work schedules. Note that managerial and sales occupations and skilled production worker[12] occupations have a higher

---

[8] ECI Collection Manual, p.68
[9] These occupations comprised an estimated 4.1 percent of US private industry employment in March 1997 and included jobs in the following occupation titles: Taxicab Drivers and Chauffeurs, Bartenders, Waiters/Waitresses, Barbers, Hairdressers and Cosmetologists, and Baggage Porters and Bellhops.
[10] Two occupations in the Managers group that have a high incidence of incentive pay are Sales Managers and Financial Underwriters.
[11] See, for example, Lettau (1997).
[12] I include as "skilled production" jobs all occupation titles that are in the following Census occupation groups: Precision Production, Craft and Repair; Machine Operators, Assemblers, and Inspectors; Transportation and Material Moving Occupations.

incidence of use of incentive pay than among all private industry jobs. Earnings and employers costs are expressed as dollars per hour worked.[13] The total employer voluntary costs measure in the second row of Table 2 is total employer costs net of payroll taxes and other mandated benefits.

Table 2 also presents data on both the incidence and generosity of supplemental compensation among jobs in the sample. Panel I of Table 2 provides summary incidence information on the types of supplemental compensation to be analyzed, the use of incentive pay, and collective bargaining coverage. Because less than 0.5 percent of employment are in jobs that have both collective bargaining and use incentive pay, the interaction between these two job characteristics was not studied. Panels II and III of Table 2 provide measures of how generous is the supplemental compensation in jobs where it is provided. Since employer costs for paid leave and overtime reflect the straight time pay rate as well as hours, I converted employer costs for both paid leave and overtime into "accrual rates"—hours accrued per thousand hours worked—by dividing these costs by the straight time pay rate.[14]. For ease of interpretation Panel III of Table 2 presents these rates as hours obtained per thousand hours of work. Using US private industry sample averages, these accrual rates imply about 155 hours of holiday and vacation leave are earned annually jobs in providing this kind of leave and about 44 hours of overtime are worked in jobs providing overtime premiums.

IV. Estimation Methodology

Expected differences in employer costs for employee compensation with use of incentive pay, controlling for other job characteristics, depend on the combined effects of the use of incentive pay on incidence and generosity. Let P_S denote the probability of a job offering supplemental compensation type S and E_S as employer expenditures per hour worked when S is offered so that expected expenditures in a sample of jobs is $P_S E_S$. Consider then the partial differentiation of $P_S E_S$ with respect to use of incentive pay.

---

[13] Hours worked is defined as the year round work schedule plus annual overtime hours less annual hours of paid leave.
[14] To obtain the overtime hours accrual rate, I divided by one and a half times the pay rate to reflect the overtime premium.

Using the log of $P_S E_S$ to emphasize relative differences and I to denote use of incentive pay, then

(I) $\quad \partial \log(P_S E_S) / \partial I = \partial \log(P_S) / \partial I + \partial \log(E_S) / \partial I.$

Thus, implicit partial (job characteristics held constant) indexes of expected relative costs of employer costs for supplemental compensation can be derived by combining estimates of incidence effects and generosity effects from use of incentive pay.

The estimation strategy follows the approach used by Freeman (1981) to analyze union-nonunion differences in supplemental compensation. Reduced-form regressions on measures of the incidence and generosity of supplemental compensation include a dummy variable indicator for whether incentive pay is used on the job along with other job characteristics. The regression coefficient on the incentive pay indicator indicates the predicted difference in supplemental compensation in the job market with use of incentive pay, holding total job compensation and other job characteristics (e.g., occupation, industry, establishment size, collective bargaining status) constant. When these predicted differences were not statistically significant, I inferred that use of the supplemental compensation did not systematically vary with use of incentive pay.

The use of incentive pay as a predetermined variable in the supplemental compensation equations can be justified in the following way. Rather than viewing the firm's use of incentive pay, the market rate of compensation for a job, and the compensation mix for a job as mutually determined it is reasonable to consider the determination of this set of variables as a recursive process. Firms choose the method of pay based on occupational characteristics, the production processes of the industry, the type of capital investment, as well as possibly many factors that are idiosyncratic to each establishment.[15] Given the firm choice of use of incentive pay, the job market matches up workers with jobs, determining compensation levels and thus also the differentials in compensation with observable job characteristics. Given use of incentive pay and total market compensation, preferences of workers for supplemental compensation and the

---

[15] For further discussion, see MacLeod and Parent (1998).

costs and benefits to firms of providing supplemental compensation determine the mix of compensation.

From this job market perspective, the estimates of (I) depend on both firm interests and worker preferences in the allocation of compensation between wage earnings and pay supplements. Thus, obtaining negative values for estimates of (I) does not necessarily imply that the use of incentive pay reduces the marginal benefit of the pay supplement to the firm, because the result may also reflect different preferences among workers in jobs using incentive pay. However, if incentive pay does reduce the marginal benefit of the pay supplement as an incentive instrument, we should never observe a positive estimate for (I). Furthermore, if a particular compensation supplement is not an incentive instrument for the firm (as would be expected for provision of health insurance, for example) there should be no differences with incentive pay unless the workers in incentive pay jobs value that particular compensation supplement differently than other workers.

If use of incentive pay were only specific to some occupations, it would be impossible to distinguish whether differences in supplemental compensation were due to method of pay rather than occupational differences. All regression equations do include indicators for the detailed occupational title (i.e., a 4-digit Census occupational code) of the sample job so that the predicted effects reflect differences with use of incentive pay within a detailed occupation.[16] This margin is empirically important because the ECI data show that detailed occupation does not determine use of incentive pay. In the ECI sample, incentive pay used for all sample jobs in only two occupations (Fishers, Hunters, and Trappers, and Hand Molding Occupations) that represent a negligible share of U.S. private industry employment. In fact, a considerable number of within-occupation comparisons can be made because the ECI sample also indicates that more than two-thirds (68.2 percent) of U.S. private industry employment is in detailed occupations that use incentive pay in some, but not all, jobs in the occupation.

---

[16] In making comparisons across all US private industry jobs, there are controls for 447 occupational titles.

ECI data collection also provides a number of other relevant statistical controls. All equations include dummy variable indicators for establishment employment size ranking and the industry of the establishment, and whether compensation of the sample job was determined through collective bargaining (union jobs). The industry classification has seventy-two indicators (essentially, a BLS variation on the 2-digit SIC classification of the employing establishment). To allow the effect of establishment size to be nonlinear, the establishment size indicator used in the regressions was the decile ranking of the establishment in the distribution of employment in U.S. private industry. To allow for possible nonlinear effects of total job compensation on worker demand for supplemental compensation, the total compensation indicator used was the decile ranking of the total compensation of the job in the distribution of total compensation across all full-time jobs in U.S. private industry.

All regression equations were least squares estimates, with adjustment of standard errors to reflect the ECI sample design. The ECI has a two stage sampling process; the establishment is the primary sampling unit with subsequent random draws of one to seven jobs from a list of all jobs employed within the establishment. Thus, regression errors across jobs within the same establishment will be correlated when firms provide the same pay supplements for all jobs in the establishment. Standard errors were estimated using Huber-White procedures, using the ECI sampling weight information and allowing for interdependence of errors between jobs sampled from the same establishment.

V. Estimated Effects of Incentive Pay and Collective Bargaining on Pay Supplements

Using a March 1997 ECI micro data cross section, estimates of (I) were obtained for expected accrual rates for hours of overtime work and holiday/vacation leave and for expected employer spending per hour worked on bonuses, health insurance, defined benefit retirement benefits, and defined contribution retirement benefits. Holding other job characteristics constant, use of incentive pay was estimated to lower both hours of overtime and hours of holiday vacation leave and also to lower employer spending on bonuses and on defined contribution retirement plans. (Estimated effects on expected employer spending on health insurance and defined benefit retirement depended on the types of occupational comparisons used; these patterns are discussed in further detail below.) Thus, use of incentive pay systematically lowers the share of total compensation derived from supplemental compensation, holding other job characteristics constant. In contrast, the presence of collective bargaining systematically raises the share of total job compensation derived from individual straight-time cash earnings because union jobs are predicted to have higher spending on all the pay supplements examined except bonuses, holding other job characteristics constant.

V.1 Incidence of Pay Supplements

Linear probability equations were used to obtain estimates of the incidence effects. Maximum likelihood (ML) techniques (e.g., a probit specification) cannot be used with large numbers of dummy variables (see Greene (1997)); in our statistical design, over five hundred dummy variables are used as statistical controls in the US private industry comparisons. (The large number of dummy variables largely reflects the controls for detailed occupation of the job, in order to make within-occupation comparisons.) Also, unambiguous comparisons of goodness of fit across equations for the different types of pay supplements studied can not be obtained with use of ML techniques (see Gronau (1998)).

Table 3 presents the results on incidence. Panel I (first three columns) provide results estimating linear probability models using all US private industry data; Panels II and III restrict the comparisons to the managerial and sales jobs data and the skilled production jobs data, respectively. The first column in each panel reports the adjusted R-square of the estimating equation and the next two columns report the estimated probability differences with use of incentive pay and collective bargaining (union job), respectively. (The effects of interactions between use of incentive pay and collective bargaining were not estimated because only 0.5 percent of all US private industry employment are in jobs with both incentive pay and collective bargaining.)

For U.S. private industry as a whole, use of incentive pay is predicted to reduce the probability of the job offering overtime work, bonuses, and paid vacation leave, with the largest estimate effect on the offer of overtime work. The predicted probability of the job offering a defined contribution retirement plan was higher among managerial and sales jobs but lower among skilled production jobs with use of incentive pay. Use of incentive pay had no statistically significant effects on the incidence of either defined benefit retirement plans or health insurance.

The estimated effects of a collective bargaining agreement--having a union job—on the incidence of pay supplements are quite different than the incentive pay effects. Having a union job has no significant effect on the offering of holiday/vacation leave or bonuses but increases the probability of the job offering overtime work, health insurance, or a defined benefit retirement plan, with the largest impact on the offering of overtime work. The predicted increase in offering a defined benefit retirement plan in union jobs reflects for the most part a substitution away from the offer of a defined contribution retirement plan. For example, in the US private industry comparisons, union jobs are predicted to have a 0.326 increase in the probability of offering a defined benefit retirement plan but also a 0.289 decrease in the probability of offering a defined contribution retirement plan.

V.2 Generosity of Pay Supplements

Table 4 presents the results for the other component of expected employer costs for supplemental compensation, how generous is the compensation where provided. The setup of Table 4 is similar to that for the incidence results in Table 3, although sample sizes vary between types of supplemental compensation because the analysis excludes jobs not offering the supplemental compensation. The generosity of overtime payments and paid holiday-vacation leave are expressed as "accrual rates"--hours per hour worked. Accrual rates are used for overtime and paid leave because costs are a direct function of straight-time earnings (one and a half times earnings for overtime pay). The equations for expenditures on supplemental compensation are in semi-log forms, so that the coefficients on the indicators for the job characteristics estimate relative differences in expenditures per hour worked.

The results in Table 4 show that when a job offers paid holiday or vacation leave, workers in jobs using incentive pay accrue fewer hours. In both the skilled production and managerial/ sales occupation groups, workers are predicted to also have less overtime work where overtime is used, although no systematic differences in overtime use were found when the comparisons were extended to all US private industry jobs. Among all US private industry jobs, spending on bonuses and defined contribution retirement is predicted to be lower with use of incentive pay, but with no systematic differences in employer spending for health insurance benefits or defined benefit retirement plans. (However, comparing among managerial and sales occupations, use of incentive pay is associated with lower employer spending on all four types of compensation supplements.)

As with the incidence effects the incentive pay differences contrast sharply with the union-nonunion differences. Workers in union jobs that offer overtime and paid leave are predicted to work more hours of overtime but also receive hours of more paid time off. The use of collective bargaining in a job is associated with no systematic differences in spending on bonuses where they are provided, but increases in employer spending on health insurance benefits. As in the case of incidence, employer spending on retirement benefits in union jobs appears to reflect in part a substitution of contributions to defined benefit retirement plans for contributions to defined contribution plans, relative to spending in nonunion jobs.

V.3 Indexes of Expected Costs for Pay Supplements

Table 5 presents antilogs of estimates of (I)--the derivatives of expected log costs, or expected hours accrued, with use of incentive pay or collective bargaining. These data reflect both incidence and generosity effects but are partial indexes because they set expected costs or hours accrued in nonunion jobs not using incentive pay to 100 hold other job characteristics constant. (Entries of 100 indicate that these job characteristics had neither a statistically significant effect on incidence or on generosity of that type of supplemental compensation.) In the comparisons across all US private industry jobs, employer costs for bonuses are about half (46.1 percent) of what they otherwise would be with use of incentive pay and about two thirds (66.94 percent) of an expected employer spending levels for defined contribution retirement. Following the consistent patterns of effects of collective bargaining on both the incidence and generosity of pay supplements, the use of collective bargaining increases the expected costs of all pay supplements except bonuses (unaffected) and defined contribution retirement plans (reduced). Reductions in spending for defined contribution retirement in union jobs reflects a substitution toward providing retirements in union jobs in traditional defined retirement benefits, which has employer spending from two to three times the level expected with nonunion jobs having similar job characteristics, depending the type of job comparison made.

VI. Conclusions: Job Characteristics and Worker Choice of Pay Supplements

To analyze how pay supplements vary in the U.S. job market this paper emphasizes the importance of the interest of the firm in employee governance. I obtained some indirect evidence on this issue by observing differences in the firm's offer of various pay supplements when the firm can use the high-powered incentives embedded in incentive pay schemes such as piece rates or commissions. As expected, use of cash bonuses not based on individual results and amount of overtime hours worked are both predicted to be lower with use of incentive pay (holding a range of other job characteristics constant). However, because use of incentive pay is also associated with differences in offers of paid leave and retirement contributions, it seems reasonable that worker preferences also play a role in these job market differences as well.

The results have some further implications about how usual hours of work vary with use of incentive pay or collective bargaining. While worker preferences between income and leisure may drive long run changes in hours at work, we rarely observe workers negotiating different hours of work within the same establishment. Uniform hours of work in the establishment helps the firm to achieve predictable work schedules and to exploit the advantages of team production.

But workers do still have a choice of work schedules through selecting different jobs. Even with wide-spread use of a standard 40 hour work week, workers can vary desired hours of work by searching for jobs with different provision of paid leave and/or utilization of overtime work; more overtime hours increase the effective work week while more paid leave reduces it. The results of this paper imply that worker choice of job with incentive pay or with a union contract can substantially change effective hours of work given the same full-time schedule. Workers with a low preference for leisure relative to income should be attracted to incentive pay jobs while workers with a high preference for leisure relative to income should be attracted to union jobs (although the results also show that more overtime hours of work are associated with union jobs).

To see how the empirical results characterize the range of choice in effective hours of work, consider worker choice between union jobs, nonunion jobs using incentive pay, and nonunion jobs without incentive pay assuming each job alternative offers both paid holiday/vacation leave and usual overtime work. What then are predicted differences in hours of work among these job alternatives from the results of this paper, holding constant other job characteristics[17] used in the statistical controls?

Table 6 provides the relevant predictions using a uniform year round 40 hours a week work schedule (2080 hours per year) and the job market sample means given for accrual rates for overtime work and paid leave given in Table 2. On average, the provision of holiday/vacation leave reduces annual hours of work in nonunion jobs not using incentive pay by about 19 days per year (155 hours per year). In contrast, the use of overtime work in these jobs increases the work year by about 44 hours per year among full time U.S. private industry jobs (but 62 hours per year in skilled production jobs). Applying the Table 4 regression estimates to these baseline estimates implies that nonunion jobs using incentive pay should have about 3 ½ less days per year (28.25 hours

---

[17] These job characteristics were: detailed occupation of the job, industry of the establishment, decile ranking of the job in the distribution of total job compensation in U.S. private industry, and decile ranking of establishment in the distribution of establishment employment size in U.S. private industry.

per year) paid leave while union jobs should have about about 2 ½ more days per year (22.18 hours per year). Thus, the results suggest that a worker choosing a job with incentive pay instead of a union job is predicted to have an effective decrease of over 50 hours of paid leave per year (among all US private industry full time jobs). Union jobs also are predicted to require more overtime work, but the increase in hours worked choosing a job with incentive pay over a union job is still more than a week a year (about 43 hours) more after netting out the additional overtime work predicted by the results for union employment. Further investigation of how these differences in hours of work influence earnings premiums in both union jobs and with use of incentive pay would be useful.

References

Barkume, Anthony J. and Thomas Moehrle, "The Impact of Incentive Pay on the Volatility of the Employment Cost Index," Compensation and Working Conditions (forthcoming 2001).

Booth, Allison L. and Jeff Frank, "Earnings, Productivity, and Performance-Related Pay," Journal of Labor Economics, vol. 17, no.3 (July 1999), pp. 447-463.

Brown, Charles, "Wage Levels and Methods of Pay," Rand Journal of Economics, vol. 23, no.3 (Autumn 1992) pp. 366-375.

Freeman, Richard B., "The Effect of Unionism on Fringe Benefits," Industrial Labor Relations Review, vol.34 (July 1981), pp.489-509.

Greene, William H., Econometric Analysis, (Third Edition) Prentice-Hall, New Jersey 1997.

Gronau, Reuben, "A Useful Interpretation of R^2 in Binary Choice Models (Or, Have we Dismissed the Good Old R^2 Prematurely?) Working Paper #397, Industrial Relations Section, Princeton University, February 1998.

Gruber, Jonathan, and Michael K. Lettau "How Elastic is the Firm's Demand for Insurance?" NBER Working Paper 8021, November 2000.

Holmstrom, Bengt and Milgrom, Paul, "The Firm as an Incentive System," American Economic Review, vol. 84 (September 1994) no. 4, pp. 972-991.

Ippolito, Richard A., Pension Plans and Employee Performance: Evidence, Analysis, and Policy. University of Chicago, 1997.

King, Sandra L, "Incentive and Time Pay in Auto Dealer Repair Shops," Monthly Labor Review, vol.98 (September 1975), pp.45-48

Lazear, Edward P., "The Power of Incentives," American Economic Review, vol.90, no.2 (May 2000), pp.410-414.

Lettau, Michael K., "Compensation in Part-time Jobs vs. Full-time Jobs: What if the Job is the Same?" Economic Letters, vol. 56 (1997), pp. 101-106.

MacLeod, W. Bentley and Daniel Parent, "Job Characteristics and the Form of Compensation," Research in Labor Economics, vol.18 (1999), pp. 177-242.

Mitchell, Daniel J. B., David Lewin, and Edward E. Lawler III, "Alternative Pay Systems, Firm Performance, and Productivity," in Paying for Productivity, Alan S. Blinder, editor, Brookings Institution, Washington, D.C. 1990, pp. 15-94.

Parent, Daniel. "Method of Pay and Earnings: A Longitudinal Analysis" Industrial and Labor Relations Review," vol. 53, no.1 (October 1999), pp.71-86.

Pencavel, John H. "Work Effort, On-The-Job Screening, And Alternative Methods of Renumeration," Research in Labor Economics: An Annual Compilation of Research, Ronald G. Ehrenberg, editor (vol. 1, 1977) JAI Press, pp. 225-258.

Petersen, Trond. "Reward Systems and the Distribution of Wages," Journal of Law, Economics, and Organization, vol. 7, Special Issue, 1991, pp. 130-158

Pierce, Brooks, "Compensation Inequality," Quarterly Journal of Economics (forthcoming, 2001).

Reisenwitz, Eric M., "Absence/Lost Time Management: Strategies to Keep the Workforce Productive," Benefits Quarterly, vol. 13 (1997), no. 4, pp.19-25

Seiler, Eric, "Piece Rate vs. Time Rate: The Effect of Incentives on Earnings" Review of Economics and Statistics, vol. 66 (August 1984), pp. 363-364.

Williamson, Oliver, Markets and Hierarchies: Analysis and Antitrust Implications New York: Free Press, 1985.

Table 1. Employer costs per hour worked for employee compensation, U.S. private industry full time jobs, March 2001

	All workers in private industry	Machine Operators, Assemblers, and Inspectors
Total Compensation	$20.81	$19.35
Wages and Salaries (includes incentive pay)	$15.18	$13.48
Benefit Costs, Total	$5.63	$5.87
Paid Leave (e.g., vacation and sick leave)	$1.37	$1.08
Supplemental Pay (e.g., overtime pay and bonuses)	$0.61	$1.00
Insurance (e.g., health insurance premiums)	$1.28	$1.57
Retirement and Savings (e.g., contributions to 401k plans)	$0.62	$0.51
Legally Required Benefits (e.g., payroll taxes)	$1.73	$1.61
Other Benefits	$0.02	$0.05

Source: Extract from Table 10 of Bureau of Labor Statistics news release "Employer Costs for Employee Compensation – March 2001" issued June 29, 2001.

Table 2. Summary Statistics (ECI samples of full time jobs in US private industry employment, March 1997)

	All private industry (N=15,257)	Managerial and Sales Occupations (N=4,172)	Production Worker Occupations (N=3,494)
Straight-time earnings (dollars per hour worked)	14.721 (10.569)	17.075 (14.711)	12.958 (5.524)
Total employer voluntary costs (dollars per hour worked)	18.938 (14.994)	21.165 (19.391)	17.003 (8.387)
I. Employment incidence in jobs:			
-with incentive pay provisions	.0784	0.174	0.094
-with collective bargaining agreement	0.139	0.037	0.269
-providing paid holiday or vacation leave	0.929	0.841	0.902
-using overtime premium payments	0.606	0.356	0.806
-paying nonproduction bonuses	0.421	0.405	0.444
-paying for health insurance	0.849	0.714	0.845
-with defined benefit pension plan	0.333	0.253	0.399
-with defined contribution retirement	0.553	0.516	0.515
II. Employer costs (dollars per hour worked) in jobs providing:			
-nonproduction bonuses	0.995 (7.301)	1.431 (4.784)	0.415 (0.674)
-health insurance	1.432 (0.979)	1.430 (0.930)	1.594 (1.121)
-defined benefit retirement	1.069 (5.156)	1.769 (12.446)	1.117 (1.210)
-defined contribution retirement	0.648 (0.918)	0.953 (1.265)	0.491 (0.660)
III. Accrual rates (hours per thousand hours worked) in jobs providing:			
Paid holiday or vacation leave	78.76 (38.77)	79.34 (39.45)	77.75 (41.77)
Work hours with overtime premium	22.28 (23.28)	15.62 (19.59)	31.36 (25.39)

Source: Job level data from the Employment Cost Index sample for March 1997; means and standard deviations (in parentheses)

Table 3. Incidence effects: predicted differences in offering pay supplements with use of incentive pay or collective bargaining agreements on pay supplement in full time jobs, March 1997

	I. All US private industry (N = 15,257)			II. Managerial and sales occupations (N = 4,172)			III. Skilled production occupations (N=3,494)		
	Adjusted R-square	Use of Incentive Pay	Collective Bargaining Agreement	Adjusted R-square	Use of Incentive Pay	Collective Bargaining Agreement	Adjusted R-square	Use of Incentive Pay	Collective Bargaining Agreement
Overtime Work	0.393	-0.1964* (0.0283)	0.1136* (0.0209)	0.382	-0.0280 (0.0496)	0.2369* (0.0561)	0.315	-0.2576* (0.0461)	0.0571* (0.0276)
Holiday or Vacation Leave	0.310	-0.0769* (0.0168)	-0.0137 (0.0112)	0.506	-0.0588 (0.0384)	-0.0536 (0.0369)	0.361	-0.0633* (0.0300)	-0.0292 (0.0171)
Bonuses	0.125	-0.1420* (0.0292)	-0.0526 (0.0308)	0.158	0.1324 (0.0709)	-0.0938 (0.0620)	0.153	-0.1019 (0.0524)	-0.0504 (0.0480)
Health Insurance	0.394	-0.0070 (0.0201)	0.0417* (0.0116)	0.428	0.0256 (0.0312)	-0.0411 (0.0299)	0.453	0.031 (0.0330)	0.0412* (0.0160)
Defined Benefit Retirement	0.388	-0.0367 (0.0367)	0.3268* (0.0285)	0.316	0.0008 (0.0606)	0.1405* (0.0591)	0.498	0.0474 (0.0417)	0.3209* (0.0435)
Defined Contrib. Retirement	0.289	-0.0452 (0.0308)	-0.2897* (0.0312)	0.275	0.1155* (0.0478)	-0.2065* (0.0643)	0.339	-0.1342* (0.0515)	-0.3050* (0.0491)

Source: Job level data from the Employment Cost Index sample for March 1997. Probabilities obtained from estimation of linear probability model. Statistical controls include: four-digit Census occupational title, two-digit SIC industry of establishment, decile ranking of the job in the US private industry distribution of total job compensation net of legally required costs, and the decile ranking of the employing establishment in the establishment employment size distribution in U.S. private industry

Table 4. Generosity effects: predicted differences in hours accrued or employer costs in jobs using compensation supplements, full time jobs, March 1997

	I. All US private industry			II. Managerial and sales occupations			III. Skilled production occupations		
	Adjusted R-square and N	Use of Incentive Pay	Collective Bargaining Agreement	Adjusted R-square and N	Use of Incentive Pay	Collective Bargaining Agreement	Adjusted R-square and N	Use of Incentive Pay	Collective Bargaining Agreement
Hours accrued:									
-Overtime Work	0.304 (N=9,127)	-0.00448 (0.00265)	0.00356* (0.00135)	0.218 (N=2,476)	-0.00532* (0.00135)	0.00883* (0.00242)	0.249 (N=3,142)	-0.01056* (0.00308)	0.00442* (0.00191)
-Holiday-Vacation Leave	0.515 (N=14,415)	-0.01435* (0.00161)	0.01127* (0.00184)	0.619 (N=4,144)	-0.01810* (0.00230)	0.01244* (0.00393)	0.596 (N=3,350)	-0.01457* (0.00304)	0.01018* (0.00312)
Log employer costs:									
-Bonuses	0.479 (N=6,823)	-0.4236* (0.1383)	-0.2368 (0.1210)	0.590 (N=1,902)	-0.4340* (0.1438)	-0.2738 (0.3599)	0.422 (N=1,619)	-0.2879 (0.1942)	-0.0760 (0.1584)
-Health Insurance	0.243 (N=13,871)	-0.0960 (0.0897)	0.3010* (0.0556)	0.251 (N=3,463)	-0.2958* (0.1312)	0.4123* (0.1845)	0.337 (N=3,093)	0.0590 (0.1421)	0.1778* (0.0802)
-Defined Benefit Retirement	0.478 (N=6,597)	-0.1240 (0.1027)	0.3605* (0.0924)	0.630 (N=1,554)	-0.2826* (0.1346)	0.3500* (0.1774)	0.571 (N=1,710)	0.0058 (0.1648)	.1772 (0.1453)
-Defined Contrib. Retirement	0.520 (N=9,678)	-0.4013* (0.0789)	-0.1768* (0.0797)	0.590 (N=2,642)	-0.5260* (0.0852)	0.0853 (0.1823)	0.503 (N=1,997)	-0.2699 (0.1857)	-0.2362* (0.1163)

Source: Job level data from the Employment Cost Index sample for March 1997. Least squares estimates with additional statistical controls for: four-digit Census occupational title, two-digit SIC industry of establishment, decile ranking of the job in the US private industry distribution of total job compensation net of legally required costs, and the decile ranking of the employing establishment in the establishment employment size distribution in U.S. private industry

Table 5. Partial Indexes of expected relative costs of pay supplements with use of incentive pay or collective bargaining

(Nonunion jobs without incentive pay and same job characteristics =100)

	All private industry		Managerial/Sales		Skilled Production	
	Use of Incentive Pay	Collective Bargaining Agreement	Use of Incentive Pay	Collective Bargaining Agreement	Use of Incentive Pay	Collective Bargaining Agreement
I. Expected accrual rates						
-Overtime Work	72.73	141.00	71.13	342.37	51.87	123.58
-Holiday-Vacation Leave	76.72	115.38	79.60	116.97	77.24	114.03
II. Expected log employer costs:						
-Bonuses	46.10	100.0	64.79	100.0	100.0	100.0
-Health Insurance	100.0	141.92	74.39	151.02	100.0	125.4
-Defined Benefit Retirement	100.0	382.62	75.38	247.27	100.0	223.50
-Defined Contrib. Retirement	66.94	49.62	73.92	67.01	77.06	43.67

Source: Antilog of estimate of Equation (I) in the text combining incidence and generosity effects reported in Tables 3 and 4.

An index value of 100 indicates that neither the incidence nor generosity effect of the job characteristic was statistically significant.

Table 6. Predicted differences in annual mean hours of paid leave and overtime with use of incentive pay and collective bargaining in US full time jobs providing these pay supplements (generosity effects), March 1997

	All Private Industry	Managerial and Sales	Skilled Production
mean hours of work[1]	1968	1955	1987
mean overtime hours[2]	43.8	30.5	62.3
mean holiday/vacation leave hours[2]	155.1	155.1	154.5
I. Predicted differences in annual hours of paid holiday or vacation leave[3]:			
-with use of incentive pay	-28.25	-35.39	-28.96
-with collective bargaining	22.18	24.32	20.23
II. Predicted differences in annual hours of overtime work[3]:			
-with use of incentive pay	0[4]	-10.40	-20.99
-with collective bargaining	7.01	17.26	8.78

Notes:
1. Mean hours of work equals 2080 hours (full time year round work schedule) plus mean overtime hours minus mean hours of holiday or vacation paid leave in Table 2.
2. Applying mean hours of work to accrual rates in Table 2
3. Mean hours of work applied to regression coefficients in Table 4.
4. A zero indicates differences were not statistically significant

www.ingramcontent.com/pod-product-compliance
Lightning Source LLC
Chambersburg PA
CBHW081417170526
45166CB00010B/3376